32 Antlers

32 Antlers

by
Jasmine Suntrell

For J.A.S. who are MINE.

Poems

I Have a Thing About Antlers Pt. I (Or Living with PCOS and Depression)

(I have a thing about antlers.)

Did you know most deer shed their antlers once a year?

(I have a thing where I lose pieces of me, periodically.)

In most species of deer, only the males have antlers at all.

(I have a thing where I don't always feel woman or man.)

A drop in testosterone triggers bucks to lose their antlers.

(I have a thing that gives me too much testosterone.)

The bone structures weaken and they lose their antlers.

(I have a thing I take that curbs my testosterone and I feel weak.)

This antler shedding begins to happen in the fall.

(I have a thing called depression that worsens in colder months.)

Rapid antler growth appears again in the summer.

(I have a thing called mania that appears with a change in weather.)

Deer will repeat this process, indefinitely, until they die.

(I have a thing about antlers.)

23 Steps to Living with Severe Depression (or how I get through when it feels impossible)

Step 1: Finally fall asleep at 3:49am.

Step 2: Wake up at 4:22am.

Step 3: Rock yourself back to sleep.

Step 4: Wake up at 6:57am and remain still so your mother still thinks you're asleep.

Step 5: Pull yourself from your bed 10 minutes after you hear her car leave.

Step 6: Do not eat breakfast.

Step 7: Do not take your medicine.

Step 8: Tweet… or check emails… or… whatever it is you can't remember that you do at this time.

Step 9: Think about taking your medicine.

Step 10: Do not take your medicine.

Step 11: Fall asleep while watching The View or Netflix.

Step 12: Wake up between 2 and 4 with the realization you did not eat and you did not take your medicine.

Step 13: Play cell phone games while you're falling asleep.

Step 14: Answer the phone cheerfully and lie to your mother. Yes, you had fruit for breakfast and lunch was delicious and yes you took your medicine. Yes, today is a better day.

Step 15: Force feed yourself an apple and the lunch you said you ate.

Step 16: Take your medicine.

Step 17: Shower.

Step 18: Do the dishes.

Step 19: Smile when your mother comes home.

Step 20: Watch the soaps with your mom while you slowly eat dinner.

Step 21: Call your boyfriend 10-15 times between 8:30pm and 3:57am.

Step 22: Remember you didn't even think about killing yourself, today.

Step 23: Finally fall asleep at 4:06 am. You've survived again.

I WILL NEVER STOP TALKING ABOUT IT

I remember when
you spread me apart, muffled
my cries with your hand.
You thrusted silence in me.
Now, I scream at every chance.

I Don't Cut, But...

I've done it again-
I've used another's body to punish myself.
I let him degrade me because
I'm too chicken to do it myself.
I don't ever touch myself.
I terrify myself.
Men made me too afraid to hold myself.

So, instead I face my demons head on
mouth on
on my back
on my side
thrusting fear in and out
but never conquering it
just myself.

They say some women use sex as a weapon
and I don't know about some
but I do
against me
before they get a chance to.

What a Concept

"To be truly happy."
That's what I listed as my ambition
under my senior high school photo.
Interesting to me how I knew back then
how difficult it would be for me to achieve.
Thirteen years later and I'm wondering
if I would even recognize happiness,
if I know what it looks like on me.

I know it used to look like
buttercups under chins
strawberry daiquiris and dumplings.
Sugar daddies eaten in secret,
magical green to red lipstick.
Screamsinging *This Little Light of Mine*
to the tune of my grandmother's smile.
And a host of other memories
and people who have died.

I've since found out that
I am not made of butter
and drive-thru daiquiri shops
don't move with you to Maryland.
My grandmother was a diabetic
as was my aunt with the lipstick
and now they both are past tense.
So, you see, I'm not willing to sing
that song I never believed in.

Mycophobia Pt. II

Me eating mushrooms
is cannibalism and
that's more death I
don't need to swallow.

Ellipses

.

..

...

....and that's all there was
or that I think there was
and then I...
I was talking to my mama
and she was crying,
she was questioning,
she was screaming,
telling me,
"You have got to start believing!"
"Don't you see girl?"
"Don't you see child?"
"You were dead but God wanted you alive."

I look around, doctors having frantic discussions
nurses taking my vitals over and over again
"Check the machine, it must have malfunctioned!"
"You don't just come back from the dead!"
My mama still crying,
asking me,
"Do you now see? You are where he wants you to be?!"

Another suicidal failure.
Or not?
Apparently, I died
but I must have not?
Is this a coma?
A super lucid dream?
I rip the IV from arm,
and watch the wound bleed.

Nothing makes any sense.
I try to ignore the clamor around me
as I attempt to digest
how I can still be here?
What happened to the cuts on my wrist?

My wrists are as unblemished
as the day I was born, and I wonder
if this is what this is?
A rebirth?

I tried to cut myself out of this world,
bleed my way into the galaxy and find Mars.
But the red planet must have said
"We don't need more bloodshed,
go back to where you belong"
Dismissed my pleas and sent me home.

And that is why I do not remember
what happened when I was "dead."
Because this is my revival
and nobody remembers being born.
We all forget how we get here.

My Serenity Poem

Tears threaten my eyes
as I realize more of my hair
has turned gray.
Signs I am getting older
which means watching more people I love die
until I finally do.

I am tired of being a mushroom;
a parasite of death.
I want to be more than some depressed girl,
anxiety ridden and scared to live.

Change terrifies me.
But it is inevitable
and it is what I need.
I cannot stop the grays from spreading
but I don't have to let my world
turn grayer with each new strand.

It's time I learn to let go of the unavoidable,
the pink and blue elephants that crowd my room.
Let them loose before they trample me.
I have got to learn to see the good in change
or be stagnant and never know what it means
to be free.

I Have a Thing About Antlers Pt. II (Deerkin)

I have a thing about antlers.
This thing that started when I fell in love with deer
one cloudless afternoon in Greenbelt park.

I have a thing about antlers.
This thing where on a particularly destructive night
a deer locked eyes with me,
staring into me the knowingness of
everything will be alright.

I have a thing about antlers.
This thing where I love deer but can't watch *Bambi*
since my grandma died and I'm no spiritual woman
but I believe my mama when she says
my grandma was the deer that one night.

I have a thing about antlers.
This thing about how they grow
and how they fall
and the non-permanence of it all.
Pain can be beautiful and pain will pass.
Antlers remind me of that.

I have a thing about antlers.
This thing where if I am to believe in other lives
or shapeshifters then I know
I am or was once a deer.
They are my kin.
Hunted and haunting,
misunderstood.

A Deer in Headlights

There is a common belief that deer are stupid.
They run in front of cars
and frequently glare right into the lights of death.
But maybe they are brave.
Maybe they know death is an inevitability
and that is why they risk life and limb
to cross the road
because none of it matters anyway
and maybe they stare into the lights
because they're alluring
or they know what's coming and
they face it head on, never afraid.
And if that's true,
there's nothing stupid about that.

For the Fat Girls

If I could sing, I would sing a song for the fat girls.
A song about the way they sexualize our thighs before 10.
A song about being picked last in gym,
your first real bra in third grade,
and being accused of asking for the attention
that makes you hate yourself for taking up so much space.

Us fast ass fat girls
who are too slow for the mile run and kickball
but grow too quick for the comfort of these dimwits
so they label us and blame us
and shame us for the bodies
we're ill-equipped to deal with.

I'd sing about being called "fine"
before ever being told you're beautiful.
About how straight A's don't distract from DD's.
You see...

I want to sing a song for fat girls.
Because I know what it means to go from
fat girl to fat woman and hold on to free.
I know what it means to always be too much
and pray to every god you've never known
that there be less of you the next time you wake.
I know what it's like to not be believed when you say
he didn't ask for your permission because
everyone assumes fat girls accept what they're given
and are ripe for the take.

I want to sing lullabies to fat girls.
Let them know,
"I got you" and "It will be alright."
You are fine, baby girl
and I ain't talking about the curve
of your behind but I mean you.

On the inside.
We gonna be alright.

14

For Rekia and Aiyana and Tanisha and Yvette and Miriam and Shelly and Aura and Darnisha and Malissa and Alesia and Shantel and Shereese and Tarika and Kathryn and Alberta and Kendra and Meagan and Jesse and...

They
did
not march
for you or
listen when us few
cried foul. Your black body bleeding
out, broken down did not move them. You are black woman.

Protect Black Girls

Protect the little black girls
because from the second we are
conceived the expectations of what
we ought to be are too heavy for
even the strongest of black mothers
to carry on top of the weight of this baby
or babies
baby girl or girls
already outcasts in this world
I'm talking black mothers who
may be dreading the thought of
knowing they will have to raise
a little black girl.

Protect our black girls
because black mothers sometimes
can't tell their daughters of their worth
because they do not know their own
and their mamas never told them neither.
So, sit still and take this hot comb
and cross your legs this way
and don't stay in the sun too long
and make sure you fix his plate
especially in front of his kinfolk
and what you won't do another will
but try not to be too willing
And always take what you are given
you can achieve more later.
Don't ask for it. Earn it.

Protect our black girls!
Black women ain't nothing but some
used to be black girls, anyway.

And let me tell you, the scars
don't necessarily fade with age.
Black women living in terror!
Black women choking on depression!
Black women shielding their rapists!
Black women protecting their abusers!
Black women, I cry for us!
I cry for we who have always lived
without proper protection
I cry for we who have always been told
there are limits to all we ever gonna be.

I love YOU, black girls!
I love YOU, black women!
I am here for US.
I stand by US.
I will always protect us.

Protect Black Girls Pt. II

Protect the little black girls
who got labeled wrong
from the second they was born-
called black boys
but they're girls
or boy and girl
nor here, nor there
just babies born.
Protect them all,
however they are.

Protect our little black girls,
don't let them cross the street alone.
Grab their hands,
keep them close to your hip,
tell them look both ways,
though you both know they face
dualities more complicated than this.

Protect our little black girls
who are told they can't wear dresses
and get called that word
that rhymes with maggot.
Throw them looks of encouragement
in crowded spaces,
provide shelter not just in bad weather
but in knowing your sunny day
might be a rainy day for a black girl
who can't share your umbrella.

Protect our little black girls,
that grow up to be sold,
beat,

murdered
and have their cold bodies told
"We told you, so."

No, we don't tell you so-
We don't tell you that you are valid.
We don't tell you that you are loved.
We don't tell you that you are us.

Please, protect our black girls
and women
and bodies that cannot
be assigned to one gender,
the ones with too many
strikes against them!

Let our sisters know,
it don't take death
for us to see them.

Dear World (PSA)

Don't
come
leaning
on black girls
when shit falls apart.
We do not exist to save you.

My Black Show

I'm gonna make a BLACK show.
And ain't ish gonna be *blackish* about my show.
We gonna have folks with long African names
never meant for colonial tongues.
AND we gonna have about five little Malaysias
and at least three kids called King.
My show gonna cast black people who look like me
and black people who don't.
We gonna show single mothers making it,
not struggling
and daddies that are involved.

In my black show,
nobody talks about color in a way to divide
only wonderment on how beautiful and expansive black is.
I want black people who don't call themselves black,
black people with thick accents,
black people uncomfortable with nigga,
flamboyant as fuck gay black folk,
less flashy gay black folk,
give me a few episodes of nothing but Studs.
Hell, I even want black conservatives.
We gonna cast black transfolk in trans roles
as well as in non-trans roles.
Because gender bias will not pop off on my black show!
My black show is big on inclusion!

But you know what my black show won't have?
Product placement, because fuck capitalism.
You know what else will be missing?
White people and other non-black people but
ESPECIALLY white people.
I don't need them to tell my black story.

They don't get to take up space in my black story.
I won't even cast them as extras down the street.
Hold your tongue about realism-
This is MY black story.

Black people gonna do regular shit in my black story.
Like, go grocery shopping and swipe the card with confidence
even if they're on food assistance.
Scratch that, everybody got enough food in my black show.
Conflicts are gonna be like,
"I can't believe Malcom kept this from me!"
"He was trying to surprise you for your birthday, LaPorcha!"
"But it was still a lie!"
Camera fades out and LaPorcha's arms are folded.

In my black show,
pain comes in the form of being rejected
and not having to wonder if you're too black or too dark.
Pain comes in the process of losing a loved one
or having to move away.

Nobody gets raped in my black show.
Nobody gets killed.
No stop and frisks.
No cops at all.
No crooked judges and politicians.
Did I mention, won't be no cops AT ALL?

And every week,
my black cast will go to sleep to
the sound of nothing
and the next week,
wake up to the brightest sunshine
and chirping of birds.

And the only moral of my black story will be
how happy we could be when we are left the fuck alone.

I Have a Thing About Antlers Pt. III (Shed)

I have a thing about antlers
where I collect them;
I mean I hoard them
and now I got too many of them.

I'm shedding them but
holding on to them-
can't convince myself to let go of them.

And I carry them
and wear them
and trip over them.
They're all around,
but I'm scared I won't know
who I am without
the weight of these memories
dragging me down.

Each antler so specific
and representative
of times no one seems to miss
but me
times no cares to remember
but me.

Somehow,
I've got to learn what it really means
to shed
and leave them there
for someone else to find
or rot and dry out
before my back exhausts
and they bury me-
bones in the ground.

My Dad's First Birthday Present to Me

November 19, 1986.
A baby girl is born,
your first daughter.
You go to the hospital to see her.
She reminds you of your mother
who's gone now and your daughter
will never know her but
then again she'll never know you.
You exit before she can learn your touch
and she never will for the next 32 years.

That was your first gift to me.
Showing me I have no choice
in how or why people leave.

What Daughters Take from Their Mothers

Jazpunzel, Jazpunzel!
Do not cut your gorgeous hair!
Leave it alone!
Let it grow!
People envy what you have!

But I defied my mother,
just the same.
And much like the fairytale,
it would seem my hair
was connected to her vitality
because soon after
she found out she had cancer.

And for the first time,
I saw my mother age.
I saw her mortality.
And her hair never grew back the same.
And the grays became more gray.
And her body much weaker than before.

I promise you,
I would have left my hair alone
if I knew my first exercise at rebellious youth
would link up with me watching
her lose the remainder of hers.

1992

I was five years old for most of '92,
so, forgive me, if my clearest memory is you.
You in the box.
I can still hear *Amazing Grace*
but it was no sweet sound
and I felt my face swell
much the same as it does right now
and the warmth of tears and snot
that quickly turn cold
the saltiness of the mixture in my mouth
the way my legs shook
just before I wriggled myself from that pew
and
"I DON'T WANT TO SEE MY GRANDMA IN THAT BOX!"
but I did.
I saw you.
I still see you.
And I ain't been right since 1992.

Boxes

I can't figure out why
the world is so determined
to put my loved ones in boxes
and keep them there but
I'm gonna find a way to get you
out of this cubic hell.

Brother,
hold on to my arm,
I will break you out of there.
I fear no judge or no man,
no task too much,
if it means unboxing you.
If it means you come home.

Haiku for ******

I never got the
chance to remember you but
I miss you the same.

Prime of Seventeen

I like to picture you at seventeen
because seventeen is a prime number
and the edge between child and adult
and also they say it's best to remember
those we've lost in their prime and
since these are made up memories
it is my artistic license to choose
a prime number as your prime
and I choose seventeen.

Whew.

Hi.
I'm your sister.
You know that.
You're older than me.
You're seventeen.
I'm twelve.
We're both young and ripe,
on the cusp of change.

In my memories I made up
you live to be 97,
another prime number
but I will always remember
you at seventeen.

The middle child,
both big and little brother.
Kind of stout,
head of curls
and a smile that
has already broken

at least ten hearts.

You're a running back
and mama hates it.
I am your biggest cheerleader
and you love it.
I paint my face,
make t-shirts,
and scream at every game.

Chuck just graduated college
and he couldn't be more proud
of his baby brother,
in the peak of teenagerdom,
a God amongst kids
ready to charge through adulthood
like it's some defensive end.

Yes, this is how I remember you.
Because I don't know you
never got the chance to
never seen you outside of a picture
but, somehow, I still really miss you
my brother.

My big little brother
that I now surpass with nearly thirty years
I love you.
I don't want to know your gravesite.
I don't want angel wings tattooed
and a RIP.
I want to remember you beautiful
youthful but grown
and happy.
The you that never got to be-

So, I remember you in your prime,
I remember you at seventeen.

Tanka for the Dead

The only thing more
certain than death is the love
I will always feel.
Death tried to rip you from me
but love saved a piece for me.

I Have a Thing About Antlers Pt. IV (Loving Me)

I have a thing about antlers.
My antlers-
my pieces of me
that are falling off of me
and I'm trying to hold steady.

I have a thing about antlers.
And I love them-
no two the same
but I find it hard to explain
to others why I surround myself
with jagged things.

Could you love all of me?
All these antlers
falling 'round my head,
wrapped up in my arms.
Could you accept them as
the parts of me
less easy to grasp?

I Want to be Loved

I want more than "wyd" texts.
I crave, "How was your day" phone calls.
I want hugs that attack me in daylight
and say, "Fuck you!" to my no PDA rule.
I want someone to tell me I'm pretty
because I don't believe in beautiful
and I want someone who knows that.

Where is the someone who can sleep past my snoring
and rub on my bad back?
The someone who gives me reason
to write happier poems?
The someone I can be annoying with on social media-
Instagram posts and Twitter engagement announcements.
Where is my partner in cornballery?

I need a he who can love me
as hard as I am on myself.
A he who can see that
I'm a marshmallow and I get softer
the more you warm me up.

I just want to be loved
in this world that seems
set on destroying me.
I need softness and
security in knowing
that there is someone
not obligated to but
choosing
to love ME.

Infatuation Situations with No Destination

You were one grade behind me
but that didn't stop you from
giving me the sweetest peck on the lips
or me from allowing you to.
Then we rolled in the grass
and our very first kiss was our last.

You looked like a baby Paul Rudd
and I was Clueless about love
but if you asked me then
I would swear it was how I felt for you.
From 3rd grade to adulthood,
you're still as handsome as ever
but you checking for me is never.

You thought my affection was insincere
that a drop in your weight
meant a drop in my disdain
but had you been paying attention
you'd have realized our potential.
Instead you listened to the doubt,
and from your heart, you cast me out.

You and me, we were kindred
and you became a refuge
that I didn't think I could know
but, perhaps we were too much for you
because you left me hanging out of the blue.

You were supposed to be my Finn
I, your Flame Princess
but just like the cartoon
we were barely more than
two awkward cuties
who paths went parallel
regardless of kisses that
made hearts swell.

You sought me out at a party
and made your way through
the herd of black men in your path.
Months later we began an affair
that lasted years before it failed
all because my skin is not pale.

You said you loved me-
that you wanted me to
carry your child but
how can I do that from
two thousand, seven hundred seventy-five miles?

Oh, but you...
You got into my head
and my bed with
a toothy smile and
a sincere desire to understand
but you can't be mine
so we exist on borrowed time.

The Dangers of Heterosexuality for Women

Picture surrender.
Weapons laid down, gates unlocked.
Small white flag in hand.
Imagine this exposure
left in the care of a man.

Militant

My dearest child,
I'm told to write a letter to anybody
and for the first time in all thirty years
of your mama's life-
she does not know what to say.

There's plenty of people I got words for
and yet this poem is still two days late.

My dearest child,
This is not how I meant to start your letter.
You might as well know now
that your mama is a mess of late starts
and unfinished endings but
I always have the best intentions.

So, I'm sorry in advance for my decisions
but please remember your mother is human.

My dearest child,
if you are to ever read this love letter
then that means you are here
and these tears that I spilled over your possibility
are a painful memory and not a haunting present.

Which means you are more than a dream
and you have made sense of my existence.

My dearest child,
I don't know the man I made you with.
Again, my apologies but I wanted you more
than I had the time to figure him out
and I knew I would love you enough for us both.

But just the same you deserve our all
so I hope your daddy is the GOAT.

My dearest child,
I usually write about niggas who could
never fulfill me the way you do.
But niggas are in abundance and there's
no guarantee I'll have you.

This is why I don't write of dreams
I'm too afraid won't come true.

My dearest child,
You are loved, however you are
and however you aren't.
I'll fight this cursed womb forever,
pleading for it to let you be.

And I will love you all my life
even if we never meet.

To My Next Ex-Boyfriend

Please make the title
of this poem a lie that
I get to laugh at.

An Honest Dating Profile

Hi, I'm Jasmine!
I'm 32-years-old.
I'm terrified of mushrooms and driving.
I'm obsessed with my mother.
I like long depression naps
and irresponsible shopping sprees
on Amazon and Forever 21.
I'm desperately seeking someone to father the child
that my body may or may not be willing to produce.
On any given night you might catch me
drinking alone and tweeting emo lyrics.
I have commitment issues,
I can't cook pancakes,
The Beatles are overrated,
and I'm allergic to fish.

AND to answer your question, I wear a F.
Yes, my titties are enormous.
No, I didn't need you to point it out.

You:
Over 6ft, black, with nice arms
and an even nicer-
you get the picture.
Thick snacks welcome.

Let's get shitfaced and eat tacos!

How do you say, "I'm flawed but love me,"
without sounding desperate and looney?

How do I summarize the different versions of me
when I'm never quite sure who I am?

How do you know when to reveal your trauma
and when you've shared too much?

How do I sell myself to people less interested in
what's going on in my head than my derrière?

I just want to say,
this is me.
I'm a mess but I'm worth it.
Take a chance on me
and let's promise to never lie.

A Push of a Pin

Hey, Love.
I'm ready for ya.
No pushing you away this time,
no more see you in another life.

I'm not scared of my uglier parts anymore.
I'm not scared that you might see me
for the confused and sometimes sloppy mess
of a girl trying hard at being a woman
that I am most days.
In fact, I hope that you do.
I want you to know all of me-
even the jagged spots that scratch
and pull on your sweaters.

Because I know you've got your shit too
and I still love you down to your
broken shards that cut me when
I pick you up.
And I'll pick you up
and patch you up
because I can't ever imagine
throwing you away.

Hey, Love.
I know you're paying attention
so I'm trying to show you
that I'm all in with ya.
If I don't let love in now, then when?
Don't want to waste no more of my life
running.

We might be prickly like cactuses
or two fine ass porcupines
but I'm laying my quills down for you
so come through.
46

Acknowledgements

I'm a firm believer that everyone deserves their flowers while they are living. This is to you, reader. Thank you for reading. Thank you for living. Thank you for loving. Thank you for existing.

I'll be honest, these acknowledgments are going to be long.

Shoutouts

Kristen Cropp – You were my first backer of my Indiegogo campaign and then you donated again. You didn't have to do that, obviously. You've been showing me support since you were ready to scrap for me in Skate Zone – I already knew I had it but you put your hard earned money where your heart is and I will never be able to thank you enough.

Kelle Maryland – My cousin/sister (wife). I won't put your government name out there (for once) but know you are appreciated and loved. We been through so much and you always come through when I need you to. Up next, I need you to publish your own book, shorty. You were always the better writer anyway.

Dwayne Lawson-Brown – You know I always struggle with what to say about you and to you because I could go on forever. You are goodness personified. To be let into your heart is an honor that I would never take for granted. You have made me a better writer and, more importantly, a better person. I hope you're proud of me.

Ian Thomas – You are living art. You have encouraged me multiple times and exposed me to other work that helped me grow as an artist. I really appreciate your support. I appreciate you.

Jordan Gran – I want to acknowledge you and thank you. We legit haven't seen each other since 8th grade and you still supported me. You said the work I put in was inspiring and I want you to know that knowing random acts of kindness still exist inspires me.

Lauren Walker & Tyra Walker-Owens – Lauren, my sister-in-law (lol), thank you first and foremost for my niece. Thank you secondly for supporting me on behalf of you and Tyra. I love you. As for Tyra, you are part of the reason I still exist. When it's hard to breathe, I breathe easier when I remember you and your sisters are in the world. You're too young to read this book right now but I hope one day it becomes one of your favorites. I love you.

Lisa Toepfert – Can you believe we made it here? We've come such a long way from me reading you my poems while you drink coffee and I tell you which boy inspired what. You always told me I could write a book. I didn't always believe you but I'm glad you always believed in me. Thank you.

Morganne Bryant – Twinnie!!! We haven't known each other long, it's true, but I thoroughly enjoy you. You remind me so much of me when I was younger but smarter and stronger. Keep growing and being you. I love you and I appreciate the support!

Luna Tenhue – Luna!!!!! My love!!! I feel so spiritually connected to you and your energy. One day I will show you the poem you inspired. You make everything lighter in a world so heavy and I thank you for being exactly who you are and always encouraging me to just be. I love you.

Shanna King – My sister in emo. Did you know you're one of the bravest people I've ever known? We've learned a lot of lessons the hard way but I hope we were able to help each other. It was dope of you to immediately lend your support even though we haven't seen each other in a while. Let's do brunch ASAP. I love you.

Anton Flowers – Mi flor! I love you to pieces! You are my baby daddy. You are the naughty angel on my shoulder. I'm so proud of the BLACK KING you are. Love you, Tonny.

Michael Jeffrey Stores – Can I find the right words? You are my best friend. I love you down to the holes in your socks. Can't nobody tell me shit about Michael Stores! And it doesn't matter that nobody will ever understand it because they're not meant to. Thank you for ALWAYS being there for me no matter what terms our relationship is on. No one I'm not blood related to has ever had my back like you. Did I mention that I love you?

Mychelle Huynh – Hey sister, girlfran. You've been riding for me and my writing since way back and now I'm finally putting out that book you've been encouraging. I want you to know I appreciate the love you and the kids have shown and you for sharing them with me. You all have made me better. I love you.

Ashley Mayho – Ashlayyyyy! Getting to know you has been nothing but positive. You are such a great person it blows my mind. Thank you for sharing your sister with me as well. She's so cute. I know you'll never stop trying to get me to move back to Louisiana and maybe you might win one day. Until then, Who dat loves you, baby? Me.

Benjamin Tasker, Jr. – Benjamin, how do I love thee! We have grown so close in adulthood. I love that I can call you pretty much whenever and you're going to answer. You always come through for me when I need it (except you won't hang out with me). You still owe me that bottle of Goose though.

Travis Curry – Travie, WE GO BACK. My eternal homecoming date! My Tamagotchi buddy! JRT unit! So many memories. I love you and I love your tummy. You're an amazing artist that people need to know (google him). I still remember that night you hit me up and told me I needed to make a poetry Instagram and write a book. Thank you for that push.

Sarah Hamilton – THANK YOU IMMENSELY FROM THE BOTTOM OF MY HEART FOR THIS BEAUTIFUL BOOK COVER AND CAPTURING WHAT I ASKED YOU TO. THANK YOU FOR SHARING SOME OF YOUR ANTLERS WITH ME.

Friends & Family

To my friends – near, far, close, extended, and ex, thank you for being a part of me and for any goodness you brought to my life. I don't care where we are in our relationship right now, if you are or were my friend, you are appreciated. Know that. Especially you, **Danielle**, primarily because I told you that I was not going to put you in these acknowledgements. You challenge me and help keep me sane. I know in my heart Jesse is proud of you.

To my family, I am nothing without you. NOTHING. Sometimes, I may feel like the black sheep or the odd one out but I know y'all love my weird ass and I appreciate that more than you could ever know. To my **first cousins**, I ride for y'all! Thank you for sharing with me the best grandmother anyone could ever ask for. Though my time with her was brief, she colored my world and I am forever grateful. To my **cousins' kids**, y'all are loved deeply. To My **Uncle Devil**, thank you for always calling me pretty. To **my aunts**, y'all are my other mothers that I could never replace. My Nana, My Friend Til The End, THE Auntie Mary, and My Fishie-Poo, you all are represented in me in the ways I move throughout the world. I don't want to exclude My Ms. Janice or My Ms. Wanda, the aunts I wasn't born with but chose. Ms. Janice, I hope you know you'll always be mine. Ms. Wanda, I hope you see me and smile. To my **nieces**: Kayla, Charity, and Tyra – you three are my purpose. I may never have a child of my own, who knows? But I know my life is fulfilled because of you three. There is almost NOTHING I wouldn't do for any of you. And I want to also thank your mothers (Michelle, Charissa, and Lauren) for raising such beautiful, smart, and talented young women. My nieces give me hope on my dreariest of days. I could go on forever but these acknowledgements are already long. To my chosen sister, **Shakira Vaughn**, where would I have been without you saving me from myself so many times? Nobody knows how hard we really rock and its nobody's business. I love you and thank you for my child(ren). To my **brothers**: Shongo, what is known does not require much speaking. Thank you for my nieces. I got mama. I got us. Don't worry too much. I love you too hard. J, never knowing you is one of my greatest sources of sadness but I hope I have honored you with my words. I hope you know you are forever loved. To **Herbert**, regardless of what you did or didn't do, you're still my father. I'm still a reflection of you. So, thank you for being a real person and for teaching me to not make excuses and own my shit.

To **Alberta Wells** aka Bayou Birdie aka Berta Mae aka my reason for breathing — my mommy. Everybody has a mother but not everyone has a good one. I have a DAMN GOOD (sorry for cursing) mother. Thank you for being patient with me, believing in me, and never giving up on me. You always think I can do better; be better. You taught me and Chuck how to love hard and ride for each other always. You taught me honesty and you're the most honest person I know. You're the reason I can't stand a lie! You are everything great I remember about MoMo and then some. If more people had mothers like you, then the world would be a better place. This is no rewriting of history! I know you have your flaws and we have been through it but you're the best person to go through it with. Don't cry! Tears do not excite me! (lol) I LOVE YOU MOMMY, ALWAYS.

To **Militant**, may we someday meet. I love you, baby.

About the Author

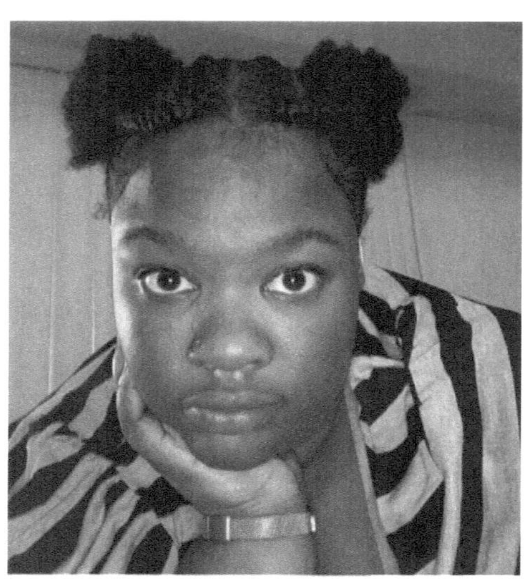

"I write poetry like prescriptions," is a quote from Jasmine Suntrell explaining her style of writing. Jasmine Suntrell is the shy poet who never performs but writes constantly. She is 32-years-old and has been dreaming up poems since she was a pre-school aged child playing in her rural Louisiana yard. An avid New Orleans Saints fan, you can find her screaming at the TV during football season. Her poetry awards are accolades from friends and teachers. She is the author of one children's book, *Finding Maw-Maw*, that only exists as one copy. Released on her 32nd birthday, *32 Antlers* is her first book of poetry. Jasmine Suntrell resides in Maryland and, while she spurns Old Bay seasoning, she loves the flag just as much as a native born Marylander. You can currently find her work at
jasminewritespoems.com
instagram.com/jasmineshortform and
facebook.com/jasminesuntrell.